MUDRAS

for

AQUARIUS

By Sabrina Mesko Ph.D.H.

The material contained in this book has been written for informational purposes and is not intended as a substitute for medical advice nor is it intended to diagnose, treat, cure, or prevent disease. If you have a medical issue or illness, consult a qualified physician.

A Mudra Hands™ Book
Published by Mudra Hands Publishing

Copyright © 2013 Sabrina Mesko Ph.D.H.

Photography by Mara
Animal photography by Sabrina Mesko
Illustrations by Kiar Mesko
Cover photo by Mara

Printed in the United States of America

ISBN-13:978-0615763705
ISBN-10: 0615763707

For all my Aquarius Friends

Table of Contents

Introduction   12
MUDRA   16
Instructions for Practice   16
Breath Control   17
Chakras   18
Nadis   21
Your Hands and Fingers   22
Mantra   22
About Astrology   23
Your Sun Sign   24
Your Rising Sign   25
How to use this book   25

MUDRAS for TRANSCENDING CHALLENGES   27
MUDRA of Divine Worship   28
MUDRA for Trust   30
MUDRA for Empowering Your Voice   32

MUDRAS for Your HEALTH AND BEAUTY   35
MUDRA for Preventing Exhaustion   36
MUDRA for Uplifting Your Heart   38
MUDRA for Strong Nerves   40

MUDRAS for LOVE   43
MUDRA for Patience   44
MUDRA for Opening Your Heart   46
MUDRA of Two Hearts   48

MUDRAS for SUCCESS   51
MUDRA for Concentration   52
MUDRA for Sharp Mind   54
MUDRA for Yin and Yang   56

About the Author   59

THE MUDRA PRACTICE IS A
COMPLIMENTARY HEALING TECHNIQUE,
THAT OFFERS FAST AND EFFECTIVE
POSITIVE RESULTS.

MUDRAS WORK HARMONIOUSLY
WITH OTHER TRADITIONAL,
ALTERNATIVE AND COMPLEMENTARY
HEALING PROTOCOLS.

THEY HELP RESTORE DEPLETED
SUBTLE ENERGY STATES
AND OPTIMIZE THE PRACTITIONER'S
OVERALL STATE OF WELLNESS.

Mudras for AQUARIUS

JANUARY 21 - FEBRUARY 18

BODY
Ankles, circulation, skin

PLANET
Uranus & Saturn

COLORS
Violet, Aquamarine, Turquoise

ELEMENT
Air

STONES and GEMS
Blue sapphire, Amethyst, Aquamarine

ANIMAL
Large Birds

Introduction

Ever since I can remember, I have been fascinated by the never ending view of the stars in the sky and the presence of other mysterious planets. As a child I wondered for hours about where does the Universe end and when my Father explained the possibility that time and space exist in a very different way than we imagined, my mind went wild with possibilities. I was however quite skeptical about astrology in general until one day in my early youth, a dear friend introduced me to a true Master of Vedic Astrology. He quickly and completely diminished any of my doubts about how precise certain facts can be revealed in one's Celestial map.

It was as if an invisible veil had been removed, and I was granted a peek over to the other side. The astrologer also adamantly pointed out that nothing is written in stone and one's destiny has a lot of space to navigate thru. You can make the best of the situation if you know your given parameters. My fascination and use of astrological science continues to this day and compliments and enriches my work with other observation techniques that I use when consulting.

One is born with character aspects and potential for realization of mapped-out future events, but there is always a possibility that another road may be taken. This has to do with the choices we make. Free will is given to all of us, even though often the choices we have seem to be very limited. But still, the choices are always there, forcing us to consciously participate and eventually take responsibility for our decisions, actions, and consequences.

The science of Astrology has been around for millenniums and even though some people are still doubtful, I always remind them that there is no disputing the fact, that the Moon affects the high and low tide of our Oceans - hence our bodies consisting mostly of water are affected by planetary movements in many fascinating and profound ways. Even the biggest skeptic agrees with that fact.

The Love of the Universal Power for each one of us is unconditional, everlasting and omnipresent. No matter what kind of life-journey you have, it is the very best one designed especially for you, rest assured. And when you are experiencing life's various challenges and wishing for a smooth ride instead, keep in mind that a life filled with lessons is a life fulfilling its purpose. The tests you encounter in your daily life are your opportunities.The wisdom learned is your asset, and the experiences gained are your wealth. Your Spirit's abundance is measured by the battles you fought and how you fought them. Did you help others and leave this world a better place in any way? Your true intention matters more than you know.

Each one of us has a very unique-one of a kind celestial map placed gently, but firmly and irrevocably into effect at the precise time of our birth. There are certain aspects of one's chart that reveal possible character tendencies and predisposed behavior in regards to love, partnerships, maintaining one's health, pursuit of success and a way of communicating. The benefits of knowing and understanding the effects of your chart on various aspects of your life can be profound. It can help you understand and prepare ahead of time for certain circumstances that are coming your way, which increases the possibility of a better quality of life in general.

If you knew that a specific time period could be beneficial for your career wouldn't it be good to know that ahead of your plans? If you are aware that certain aspects of your physical constitution are predisposed to a weakness or sensitivity, wouldn't it be beneficial to pay attention and prevent a possible future health ailment?

If you can foresee that a certain time will be slower for you in achieving positive results, wouldn't it be wise to use that time for preparation for a more fortuitous timing? How many times have you attempted to pursue a dream of yours that just didn't seem to want to happen? And when you were completely exhausted and disillusioned, the fortunate opportunity presented itself, except now you were tired, overwhelmed and had no energy or enthusiasm left. Having such information ahead of time would offer you the chance to save your energy during quiet, less active time, so that when your luck is more likely, you can seize the opportunity and make the most of it. Since writing my first books on Mudras a while ago, my work has expanded into many different areas, however I always included Mudras into my new ventures. When I designed International Wellness and Spa centers, I included Mudra programs to share these beneficial techniques with a wide audience. I included Mudras into my weekly TV show and guided large audiences thru practice on live shows.

Mudras will forever fascinate me and I have been humbled and excited how many practitioners from around the world have written me, grateful to have these techniques and most importantly really experiencing positive effects in time of need. Therefore it has been a natural idea for me to combine these two of my favorite topics and create a series of Mudra sets for all twelve Astrological signs.

The Mudras depicted in this book are specifically selected for the astrological sign of Aries with intention to help you maximize your gifts and soften the challenges that your celestial map contains.

It is important to know that each astrological chart - celestial map-contains information that can be used beneficially and there are no "bad signs" or "better sings". Your chart is unique as are you. By gaining information, knowledge and understanding what the placements of the planets offer you, your path to self knowledge is strengthened.

I hope this book will attract astrology readers as well as meditation and yoga practitioners and help you utilize the beneficial combination of both these fascinating techniques. Knowledge will help you experience the very best possible version of your life. The biggest mystery in your life is You. Discover who you are and enjoy the journey.

And remember, no matter what life presents you with, don't forget to smile and keep a happy heart. With each experience gained you are spiritually wealthier for it. And that my friend, stays with you forever.

The wisdom gained is eternally imprinted in your soul.

Blessings,

Sabrina

MUDRAS

Mudras are movements involving only fingers, hands and arms. Mudras originated in ancient Egypt where they were practiced by high priests and priestesses in sacred rituals. Mudras can be found in every culture of the world. We all use Mudras in our everyday life when gesturing while communicating and when holding our hands in various intuitive positions. Mudras used in yoga practice offer great benefits and have a tremendously positive overall effect on our overall state of well-being. By connecting specific fingertips and your palms in various Mudra positions, you are directly affecting complex energy currents of your subtle energy body. As numerous energy currents run thru your brain centers, Mudras help stimulate specific areas for an overall state of emotional, physical and mental well being.

INSTRUCTIONS FOR MUDRA PRACTICE

YOUR BODY POSTURE
During the Mudra practice sit in an upright position with a straight spine, with both your feet on the ground or in a cross legged position. Comfort is essential so that you may practice undisturbed and focus on proper practice positions.

YOUR EYES
Keep your eyes closed and gently lightly lift the gaze above the horizon.

WHERE
For achieving best results of ideal Mudra practice it is essential that you find a peaceful place, without distractions. Once your Mudra practice is established,   you can practice Mudras anywhere.

WHEN
You may practice Mudras at any time. Best times for practice are first thing in the morning and at bedtime. Avoid practicing Mudras on a full stomach, and after a big meal wait for an hour before practice.

HOW LONG
Each Mudra should be practiced for at least 3 minutes at a time. Ideal practice is 3 Mudras for 3 minutes each with a follow up short 3 minutes of complete stillness, peace and meditation or reflection.

HOW OFTEN
You may practice Mudras every day. Explore various Mudras by selecting a Mudra that fits your specific needs for any given day.

BREATH CONTROL
Proper breathing is essential for optimal Mudra practice. There are two main breathing techniques that can be used with your practice.

LONG DEEP SLOW BREATH
Slowly and deeply inhale thru your nose while relaxing and expanding the area or your solar plexus and lower stomach. Exhale thru the nose slowly while gently contracting the stomach area and pulling your stomach in. Pace your breathing slowly and notice the immediate calming effects. This breathing technique is appropriate for relaxation, inducing calmness and peace.

BREATH OF FIRE
Inhale and exhale thru the nose at a much faster pace while practicing the same concept of expanding navel area and contracting with each exhalation. Unless otherwise noted Mudras are generally practiced with the long slow breath.The breath of fire has an energizing, recharging effect on body and is to be used only when so noted.

Chakras

Along our spine, starting at the base and continuing up towards the top of your head, lie subtle energy centers-vortexes-called charkas, that have a powerful effect on the overall state of your health and well being.
The practice of Mudras profoundly affects the proper function of these energy centers and magnifies their power.

Our subtle energy body is highly sensitive to outside sensory stimuli of sound, aromas, visuals and outside electric currents that constantly surround us. Frequencies that permeate specific locations may attract or bother you. Perhaps you may feel eager to stay somewhere where the energy suits you and yet feel suffocated when the environment does not agree with you. We are all sensitive to energies, but some of us feel them more than others.

A positive blend of energies with another person can create a magnet-like effect, whereas another person's negative unharmonious subtle energy field subconsciously pushes you away.

By leading healthy lives and optimizing the proper function of charkas, you empower your subtle energy bodies adding strength to your physical body, mind and spirit. Destructive behavior like addictions and abuse weakens your Auric field and "leaks" your vital energy. By maintaining a healthy Aura-energy field, you can fine-tune your natural capacity for "sensing" places, situations and people that compliment your energy frequency.
In a state of "clean energy" you achieve capacity for high awareness and become your own best guide.

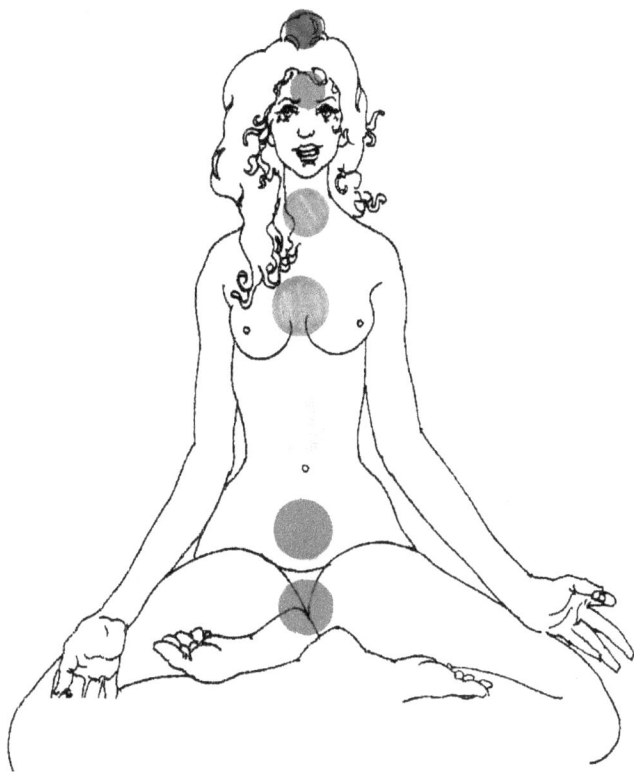

CHAKRAS IN THE BODY

Base Chakra: Foundation
Second Chakra: Sexuality
Third Chakra: Ego
Fourth Chakra: Love
Fifth Chakra: Truth
Sixth Chakra: Intuition
Seventh Chakra: Divine Wisdom

FIRST CHAKRA
LOCATION: Base of the spine
GLAND: Gonad
COLOR: Red
REPRESENTS:
Foundation, shelter, survival,
courage, inner security, vitality

SECOND CHAKRA
LOCATION: Sex organs
GLAND: Adrenal
COLOR: Orange
REPRESENTS:
Creative expression, sexuality,
procreation, family

THIRD CHAKRA
LOCATION: Solar plexus
GLAND: Pancreas
COLOR: Yellow
REPRESENTS:
Ego, intellect, emotions of fear and anger

FOURTH CHAKRA
LOCATION: Heart
GLAND: Thymus
COLOR: Green
REPRESENTS:
All matters of the heart, love,
self–love, compassion and faith

FIFTH CHAKRA

LOCATION: Throat
GLAND: Thyroid
COLOR: Blue
REPRESENTS:
Communication, truth,
higher knowledge, your voice

SIXTH CHAKRA

LOCATION: Third Eye
GLAND: Pineal
COLOR: Indigo
REPRESENTS:
Intuition, inner vision, the Third eye

SEVENTH CHAKRA

LOCATION: Top of the head - Crown
GLAND: Pituitary
COLOR: White and Violet
REPRESENTS:
The universal God consciousness,
the heavens, unity

NADIS

Your subtle energy body contains an amazing network of electric currents called Nadis. There are 72.000 energy currents that run throughout your body from toes to the top of your head as well as your fingertips. These channels of light must be clear and vibrant with life force for your optimal health and empowerment. With regular Mudra practice you can open, clear, reactivate and re-energize your energy currents.

Your Hands and Fingers

While practicing Mudras you are magnifying the effects of the Solar system on your physical, mental and spiritual body. Each finger is influenced by the following planets:

THE THUMB - MARS

THE INDEX FINGER - JUPITER

THE MIDDLE FINGER - SATURN

THE RING FINGER – THE SUN

THE LITTLE FINGER - MERCURY

MANTRA

Combining the Mudra practice with appropriate Mantras magnifies the beneficial effects of these ancient self-healing techniques.

The hard palate in your mouth has 58 energy meridian points that connect to and affect your entire body.

By singing, speaking or whispering Mantras, you touch these energy points in a specific order that is beneficial and has a harmonious and healing effect on your physical, mental and spiritual state.

The ancient science of Mantras helps you reactivate nadis, magnifies and empowers your energy field, improves your concentration and stills your mind.

About Astrology

The word Horoscope   originates from a Latin word ORA–hour and SCOPOS–view. One could presume that Horoscope means "a look into your hour of birth". The precise moment of your birth determines your celestial set-up.

An accurate astrological chart can reveal most detailed aspects of your life, your character, your gifts, your future possible events, challenges that await you, lucky events that are bestowed upon you, and your outlook for happy relationships, successful careers, accomplishments, health and many possible variations of life events. I say possible, because your decisions will determine the outcome.

There are 12 signs in the Zodiac and your birth-day reflects the position of your Sun sign. The specific positions of other planets in your chart are calculated considering the precise moment-hour and minute and of course location of your birth. The birth time will reveal your Rising or Ascending sign, which will further determine other essential facts of your chart.

The constant transitional movements of the Planets affect each one of us differently, a time that may be difficult for some may prove supremely lucky for another and yet we are interconnected by mutual effects of continuous planetary movements. Nothing is standing still, the changes are ongoing. On a different note, a few slow moving planets connect us in other ways, as they keep certain generations under specific aspects and influences. We are all inseparable and in continuous motion.

There are numerous fascinating ways to use astrology and there is no doubt that the constant motion of all these powerful and majestic Planets in our Solar system affect each and every one of us differently. Astrology can be used as an additional tool to help you continue progressing on the mysterious life journey of self discovery and self-realization.

Remember, the power of decision is yours as is the responsibility for consequences. Make peace with your doubts, pursue your dreams and relish in results.

When the outcome is less than what you expected, learn to pick yourself up and continue on, wiser with knowledge you gained, that alone being a good reason for remaining optimistic. When the outcome surpasses your expectations, well, then you will know what to do…mostly take a breath, smile, and enjoy the moment.

YOUR SUN SIGN

There are 12 signs in the Zodiac. The day of your birth determines your Sun-sign. Most often this is the extent of average person's knowledge and interest in astrology. However, the other aspects in the astrological chart are equally as important and need to be taken into consideration. In this book your main guide is your Sun sign's dispositions, tendencies, weaknesses and gifts. Certainly there are endless combinations of charts and your Sun sign alone will not reveal the complete picture of your celestial map.

For more detailed information and reflection about your chart, you need to know your ascending-rising sign.

Your Ascending-Rising Sign

Your rising sign, also known as the ascendant, reflects the degree of ecliptic rising over the eastern horizon at the precise moment of your birth. It reveals the foundation of your personality. That means that even if you have the same birthday with someone else, your time of birth would create completely different aspects and influences in your chart. No two people are alike. You are one of a kind and so is everyone else. However, you may have some strong similarities and timing aspects that will be often alike. Your rising sign also reveals the basis of your chart and House placements. Your rising sign determines and is in your first house. There are 12 Houses and each depicts precise in-depth information about all aspects of your physical life, emotional make and character tendencies. It is incredibly complex and fascinating. Regarding your Mudra practice in combination with your Astrological Sign, it would be beneficial to know also your Rising sign and apply Mudras that empower your Rising sign as well. For example; if your Sun sign is Aquarius, but your rising sign is Libra-it would be most beneficial to practice Mudra sets for both signs.

How to use this book

In each book of the *Mudras for the Astrological Signs* series, you will find Mudras for different astrological signs that will help you in most important areas of your life: Health, Love, Success, and Overcoming your challenging qualities. We all have them, as we also all have gifts. This book is specific for the sign of Aries. You may change your Mudra practice daily as needed, and keep in mind, that certain habits or tendencies need a longer time to adjust, change, and improve. Be patient, kind, and loving towards yourself.

Mudras for Transcending Challenges

Each one of us has a few character tendencies or weaknesses that are connected to our astrological chart. To help you transcend, overcome and redirect these challenges into your beneficial assets, you can use the Mudras in this chapter.

Mudras for Health and Beauty

Each astrological sign rules certain areas of your body. The Mudras in this chapter will help you strengthen your physical weaknesses while maintaining a healthy body, and a beautiful, vibrant appearance.

Mudras for Love

The Mudras in this chapter will help you understand your love temperament, your expectations, your longings and how to attract the optimal love partner into your life. It is most beneficial to know how others perceive you in the matters of the heart. It will also help you understand your partner and their astrologically influenced love map.

Mudras for Success

The Mudras in this chapter will offer you tools to present yourself to the world in your optimal light. Often one is confused in which direction to turn or where their strength lies. Mudras will help you focus and remember your essential creative desires, help you gain self-confidence and inner security to recognize your desired and destined path. If you know what you want, and your purpose is harmonious for the better good of all, your success is within reach.

MUDRAS
for TRANSCENDING
CHALLENGES

MUDRA OF
DIVINE WORSHIP

It is no secret that you want to save the world and every living specimen in it. You sense and feel what the future will bring and are perpetually ahead of your time. Your incredibly busy mind is working overtime on all channels. Before you become completely overwhelmed with various rescuing missions, remember there is a Universal guiding source that protects each and every one of us, including you. Connect with that source on a daily basis and your load will lighten considerably. After all, you are supposed to enjoy life as well.

CHAKRA: ALL

COLOR: ALL

MANTRA:

EK ONG KAR

(One Creator, God is One)

Sit with a straight back, place both palms together in front of your chest. Concentrate on your breath and gently focus your gaze on your Third eye.

BREATH: Long, deep and slow.

MUDRA FOR TRUST

It is true that you may have the capacity to get things done faster that the rest of us, but that does not mean you have to do everything yourself. Be open to receiving help, it will help you focus on things of most importance that truly only you can accomplish. It is not easy to trust others with your heart driven projects, but you should be able to trust the Universe that it will guide you on your mission and will bring you others who are of the same energy and heart. Trusting the Universe is as important as every breath you take. So relax and practice this Mudra, and feel the pressure disappear with each breath.

CHAKRA : 7

COLOR: Violet

MANTRA:

HAR HAR HAR WAHE GURU
(God's Creation, His Supreme Power and Wisdom)

Sit with a straight back, lift up your arms and create a circle with arms arched above head. Palms are turned down, women place right palm over left, men left palm over right. The thumb tips are pressed together lightly. Close your eyes and visualize a protective circle of white healing light all around you.

BREATH: Fast breath of fire from the point of your navel.

MUDRA for EMPOWERING Your VOICE

As a born peacemaker you are well aware of the importance and power of words. Your diplomatic speaking talents are under constant scrutiny and pressure. You need to be able to concentrate with ease, so you can get to the point in the shortest time possible, before the peace talks time expires and everyone's attention is gone. This Mudra will help you speak with power and conviction so that you will successfully project your message to a wide audience and accomplish your mission.

CHAKRA: 5

COLOR: Blue

Sit with a straight back, bend your elbows and lift them parallel to the ground, while you lift your hands in front of you at the level of your throat. Turn the right palm outward and the left palm towards you. Bend your fingers and hook them together, while pulling them apart. Keep your shoulders down while applying pressure to the pull.

BREATH: Long deep and slow.

MUDRAS
for HEALTH
and BEAUTY

MUDRA for PREVENTING EXHAUSTION

You rarely allow yourself the time for rest and relaxation, and now it is time to do just that. Your vulnerable area of ankles may get accident prone if you are exhausted and keep going without a break. Take care and caution and do not overextend yourself. Make regular time for letting go and replenishment of your strong physical energy battery. This Mudra will create a perfect opportunity for "hands on" relaxation and a much needed break.

CHAKRA : 3, 4

COLOR: Yellow, Green

MANTRA:

SAT NAM
(Truth is God's Name, One in Spirit)

Sit with a straight back, lift up your arms and grasp your earlobes with the thumb and index fingers. Hold your earlobes tightly and let the full weight of your arms pull on them. Relax and enjoy the immediate effects.

BREATH: Long, deep and slow.

MUDRA FOR
UPLIFTING YOUR HEART

Being that you are such an active thinker, sometimes presents a challenge. You forget about yourself. Try to remember the health of your heart is important as well. The reality is, that you can not always save everyone. This world is a learning experience and everyone needs to go thru it at some time or another. And while you understand this, you do not like it and in brings you unhappiness. This Mudra will help you uplift your heart, so that you may masterfully find the perfect balance of mind and heart. This way, when you successfully accomplish a challenging project, you will actually recognize it, and feel happy in your heart as well. Tomorrow is another day.

CHAKRA : 4

COLOR: Green

Sit with a straight back, elbows bend and parallel to the ground. Tuck your thumbs under your armpits and keep the rest of your fingers straight and together, palms facing down. The middle finger fingertips are touching, but with each inhale they separate, while with each inhale they touch or cross each other. Focus on expanding your chest and opening your heart area.

BREATH: Long, deep and slow.

MUDRA FOR
STRONG NERVES

The high responsibilities that you carry is a scenario that you create, are capable of seeing thru, and actually enjoy, but you must remember that your nervous system can suffer consequences of overload. This can result in nervous sensitivity and skin ailments. Make an effort to relax your schedule a bit, take a break, and take care of your basic needs like sleep, diet and complete relaxation. To prevent a work overload and suffer consequences, practice this Mudra and preserve your nerves. You have many goals and projects to accomplish, so pace yourself and protect your health assets. You will see what a difference it will make if you replenish your energy and take a few steps back. With some distance and air, your mind will be even more in tune. They sky is the limit.

CHAKRA : 3, 4

COLOR: Yellow, Green

Sit with a straight spine and lift your left hand to ear level with palm facing out. Connect the thumb and the middle finger while keeping the other fingers straight. The right hand is in your lap with thumb and little finger touching palm facing up towards the sky. The rest of the fingers are stretched. **The position is REVERSED for men.**

BREATH: Inhale long, deep and slow thru your nose in four counts and exhale in one strong breath.

MUDRAS
for LOVE

MUDRA for PATIENCE

Yes, you may know at first glance when you meet the love of your life, but not everyone is that fast. You may frighten your love away, if you come bulldozing in-full-force and are ready to elope within five minutes of meeting. Be tactful with your words and do not reveal your heart immediately. If you do, it may take your conquest a few weeks to recover and find the courage for the next date with you. By then you will have suffered thru massive frustration. Be patient and considerate. This Mudra will help you ease and tame your impatient nature and redirect your energy into a calmer more productive approach. You may jump into water fast, but take a nice easy swim first before you take over the sailboat and kidnap it for life.

CHAKRA : 6,7

COLOR: Indigo, White

MANTRA:

EK ONG KAR SAT NAM GURU PRASAAD
(One creator, Illuminated by God's Grace)

Sit with a straight back, lift your hands up to shoulder level and keep elbows nice and high – level with the shoulders. Connect the thumbs and the middle fingers on both hands and stretch the rest of the fingers. Your hands are at the level of your ears, palms facing out and fingers nice and stretched towards the sky.

BREATH: Long, deep and slow.

MUDRA FOR OPENING YOUR HEART

When you are dealing with the matters of love, it is time to redirect your intense focus and open your heart to show the softer, gentler side of your personality. Infuse some of that energy in your work when saving the world and nature and your will attract a more loving crowd of supporters. When communicating with your lover, melt into the softie that you are and expose your vulnerable side as well. Otherwise they will completely miss that quality in you, and fear that you are cold-hearted when in fact your mind is just intensely greedy for your attention. Your heart needs to take center-stage position, and the time is now.

CHAKRA : 4

COLOR: Green

MANTRA:
SAT NAM
(Truth is God's Name, One in Spirit)

Sit with a straight spine and lift your hands in front of your heart with palms and fingers open as if creating a cup. Keep all the fingers stretched and feel the healing energy pouring into your fingertips and the area of your heart.

BREATH: Long, deep and slow.

MUDRA OF TWO HEARTS

It is not easy to love such an independent and freedom loving person as yourself. But each love relationship involves both people and it is important that you remember this. So when you make an unexpected plan to run alone and free along the ocean for a bit, it would be wise to inform your lover. They will still love you, but it will help them understand that your excursion has nothing to do with them, you just needed some fresh air. That way, there will be no hurt feelings and nothing to explain later and you will have the feeling or air and free space between you two, even though you are inseparably madly in love. By being considerate, you will have a good chance to enjoy this earthly love, not just the "out of this world" wild fantasy that you dream about. You are here in this world right now, so might as well enjoy earthly love. You can visit other planets another time.

CHAKRA : 4

COLOR: Green

MANTRA:
SAT NAM
(Truth is God's Name, One in Spirit)

Sit with a straight spine. Connect the thumbs and index fingers on each hand and spread out and extend all other fingers. Lift your arms in front of your heart, cross arms in front of you - left in front of right, palms facing out and little fingers hooked onto each other. Keep fingers nice and extended thru the practice.

BREATH: Inhale long, deep and slow.

MUDRAS for SUCCESS

MUDRA FOR CONCENTRATION

You enjoy tremendous satisfaction when your efforts are rewarded, and you can see the fruits of your hard labor. However, your creative ideas run so wild that it is essential for you to be able to focus and concentrate on one specific area at a time. Become a true Aquarian master of the oceans and know how to navigate the waters of your wild inner oceans of creativity and invention. This Mudra will help you achieve a high level of concentration, while keeping your eye on the target.

CHAKRA : 3, 4, 6

COLOR: Yellow, Green, violet

MANTRA:

AKAL AKAL AKAL HARI AKAAL
(Immortal Creator)

Sit with a straight back. Curl each index into the thumbs and stretch the other fingers. Bring your hands up above navel area and place the backs of palms together-back to back. Palms are facing out. Keep the stretched fingers pointed up towards the sky and feel the stretch in your wrist and palm area.

BREATH: Long, deep and slow.

MUDRA FOR
A SHARP MIND

Multi tasking is a fun past time for you and you love to juggle a multitude of projects at once. However, you are still human and sometimes your brain can go into overdrive. Learn to experience different phases of your creative spells. The proper distance is required sometimes to observe the project from a different perspective. This will prove very valuable. During those rare quiet moments of reflection, practice this Mudra. It will help you maintain a razor sharp edge and stay ahead of the curve, which is where you feel right at home and in your comfort zone.

CHAKRA : 3, 6

COLOR: Yellow, Indigo

MANTRA:
HARA HARE HARI
(The Creator in Action)

Sit with a straight spine. Hold the left hand up in front of you chest as if ready to clap, then with an extended index and middle finger of your right hand firmly walk up the center of the left palm, starting at the bottom of the palm and continuing to the very tips of middle and ring fingers of the left hand. Walk up and down your palm while maintaining pressure.

BREATH: Long, deep and slow.

MUDRA FOR BALANCING
THE YIN AND YANG

Do not get discouraged if others can't follow your world-saving actions quite as fast as you would like. Every flower needs time to grow, push a bud and then finally bloom in full glory. Be aware that this world is full of contradictions and opposites, and remember that with your determined vision and devoted purpose for a better world, you will see it thru with patience and in harmony with everyone and everything. Perhaps during a moment of apparent set-back you will be gifted with another element that will truly infuse your work with magic. This will bring you immense sense of fulfillment, purpose and destiny.

CHAKRA : All

COLOR: All

MANTRA:
OM
(God in His Absolute State)

Sit with a straight spine. Connect the index and thumb fingers and extend the rest of the fingers. Lift your right hand in front of your chest with palm turned out and hold the left hand below in front of your stomach area, palm turned inward. Connect the thumbs and index fingers of both hands creating the Wheel of life.

BREATH: Long, deep and slow.

ABOUT THE AUTHOR

SABRINA MESKO PH.D.H. is an International and Los Angeles Times bestselling author of the timeless classic *Healing Mudras - Yoga for your Hands* translated into fourteen languages. She authored over twenty books on Mudras, Mudra Therapy, Mudras and Astrology, Holistic Caregiving, Spirituality and Meditation techniques.

Sabrina holds a Bachelors Degree in Sensory Approaches to Healing, a Masters in Holistic Science, a Doctorate in Ancient and Modern Approaches to Healing, and a Ph.D.H in Healtheoloyy from the American Institute of Holistic Theology. She is board certified from the American Alternative medical Association and American Holistic Health Association. She has been featured in media outlets such as The Los Angeles Times, CNBC News, Cosmopolitan, the cover of London Times Lifestyle, The Discovery Channel documentary on Hands, W magazine, First for Women, Health, Web-MD, Daily News, Focus, Yoga Journal, Australian Women's weekly, Blend, Daily Breeze, New Age, the Roseanne Show and various international live television programs. Her articles have been published in world-wide publications. She hosted her own weekly TV show educating about health, well-being and complementary medicine. She is an executive member of the World Yoga Council and has led numerous international Yoga Therapy educational programs. She directed and produced her interactive double DVD titled *Chakra Mudras* - a Visionary awards finalist.

Sabrina also created award winning international Spa and Wellness Centers and is a motivational keynote conference speaker addressing large audiences all over the world. She is the founder of Arnica Press, a boutique Book Publishing House. Her mission is to discover, mentor, nurture and publish unique authors with a meaningful message, that may otherwise not have an opportunity to be heard. She is the founder of world's only online Mudra Teacher and Mudra Therapy Education, Certification and Mentorship program, with her certified therapists spreading these ancient teachings in over 28 countries around the world.

www.SabrinaMesko.com

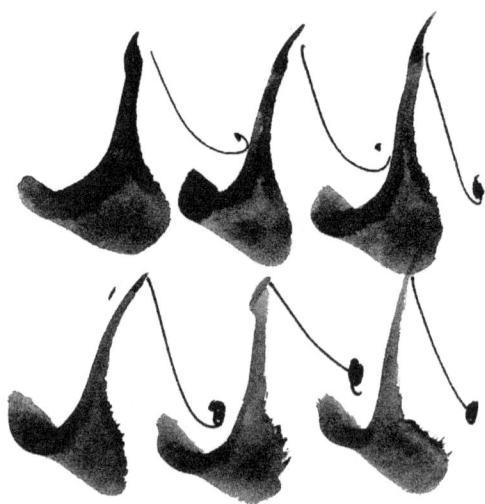

www.ingramcontent.com/pod-product-compliance
Lightning Source LLC
Chambersburg PA
CBHW071430040426
42445CB00012BA/1333